Arctic Poems

Also available in this series

Poetry

Selected Poems

Adam / Adán
Square Horizon / Horizon carré
Equatorial & other poems
Arctic Poems / Poemas árticos
Painted Poems
Paris 1925: Ordinary Autumn & All of a Sudden / Automne régulier & Tout à coup
Altazor
Skyquake / Temblor de cielo
Citizen of Oblivion / El ciudadano del olvido
Seeing and Touching / Ver y palpar
Last Poems / Últimos poemas
Uncollected Poems / Poemas inéditos

Fiction

El Cid / Mío Cid Campeador
Cagliostro
Three Huge Novels / Tres novelas inmensas
Papa, or The Diary of Alicia Mir / Papa, o el diario de Alicia Mir
Satyr, or The Power of Words / Sátiro, o el poder le la palabra

Other Prose

Manifestos
Adverse Winds / Vientos contrarios

Volodia Teitelboim: *Vicente Huidobro — in perpetual motion: A Biography*

Not all of these had yet been published when this volume went to press.
The programme should be complete by 1927.

Vicente Huidobro

Arctic Poems
Poemas árticos

Translations by
Tony Frazer

Shearsman Books

This second edition published in the United Kingdom in 2025 by
Shearsman Books
PO Box 4239
Swindon
SN3 9FN

Shearsman Books Ltd Registered Office
30–31 St. James Place, Mangotsfield, Bristol BS16 9JB
(this address not for correspondence)

www.shearsman.com

ISBN 978-1-84861-993-7

Translations and editorial matter copyright © Tony Frazer, 2019, 2025.

The right of Tony Frazer to be identified as the translator
of this work has been asserted by him in accordance with the
Copyrights, Designs and Patents Act of 1988.
All rights reserved.

Poemas árticos was originally published in Madrid in 1918 by
Imprenta Pueyo. The texts here are largely based on that edition
— see the Appendix for further details.

This edition of *Arctic Poems* replaces the first edition from 2019.

CONTENTS

	Introduction	7
12	Horas / Hours	13
14	Exprès / Express	15
18	Noche / Night	19
20	Alerta / Alert	21
22	Camino / Road	23
24	Emigrante à America / Emigrant to America	25
26	Cantar de los cantares / Song of Songs	27
28	Astro / Star	29
30	Niño / Boy	31
32	Casa / House	33
34	Ruta / Route	35
36	Gare / Station	37
38	Égloga / Eclogue	39
42	Balandro / Yacht	43
44	Invierno / Winter	45
45	Hijo / Son	47
48	Horizonte / Horizon	49
52	Vermouth / Vermouth	53
56	Llueve / Raining	57
60	Adiós / Farewell	61
64	Luna / Moon	65
66	Cruz / Cross	67
68	Osram / Osram	69
70	Paquebot / Packet Boat	71
72	Marino / Sailor	73
74	Cenit / Zenith	75
76	Nadador / Swimmer	77
78	Cuatro / Four	79
80	Départ / Departure	81
82	Donjon / Dungeon	83
84	Cigarro / Cigar	85
86	Luna o reloj / Moon or Clock	87

88	Primavera / Springtime	89
90	Eternidad / Eternity	91
92	Campanario / Bell Tower	93
94	Universo / Universe	95
96	En marcha / Under Way	97
98	Sombra / Shadow	99
100	Bay Rum / Bay Rum	101
102	Wagon-lit / Wagon-lit	103
104	Puerto / Harbour	105
106	HP / HP	107
108	Vaso / Glass	109
112	Mares árticos / Arctic Seas	113

French Versions

116	Maison / House	117
118	Gare / Station	119
120	Balandre / Yacht	121
122	Fils / Son	123
124	Lune / Moon	125
126	Cigare / Cigar	127
128	Éternité / Eternity	129
130	Clocher / Bell Tower	131
132	En marche / Under Way	133
134	Ombre / Shadow	135
136	Bay rum / Bay Rum	137

Bibliography	138
Publication History of the French Versions	138
A Note on the Texts	139

VICENTE HUIDOBRO
AND ARCTIC POEMS

Huidobro (1893–1948) published *Poemas árticos* in Madrid in 1918, this being the last of a rapid series of publications which established him as a major new talent both in French and in Spanish.[1] In the period 1917–1918, his publications were: *Horizon carré* (Square Horizon, in French; Paris, 1917), *El espejo de agua* (Mirror of Water, in Spanish; Madrid, 1918) *Tour Eiffel* (Eiffel Tower, in French; Madrid, 1918), *Hallali* (in French; Madrid, 1918); *Ecuatorial* (Equatorial, in Spanish; Madrid, 1918) and the present volume, likewise published in Spanish in Madrid. These publications mark the beginning of the author's engagement with the European avant-garde, and a transition away from the symbolist style (in Spanish, *modernista*, not to be confused with Anglo-Saxon modernism) that had dominated his writing prior to his move to Europe. The immediately preceding volume, *Adán* (Adam; Santiago, 1916; written 1914), is very much a transitional work, showing a number of somewhat undigested influences, and perhaps a little intellectual posturing by the author. By contrast, *El espejo de agua*,[2] is a kind of "bridge" volume to the new style. The appearance of the latter volume in Madrid, apparently out of sequence, might serve to confuse one's appreciation of the development of his work, but many of the poems had already turned up in *Horizon carré* in French versions, albeit organised differently on the page. Huidobro continued to rate this book, and selected work from it for subsequent compilations, including his French-language selected poems, *Saisons choisies* (Selected Seasons; Paris, 1921).

Poemas árticos is particularly interesting in that it shows the author bringing into Spanish the lessons he had learned (and already deployed in *Horizon carré*) from Apollinaire and Reverdy—friends from his earliest days in Paris. This book, together with the chapbooks, *Ecuatorial*, *Hallali* and

---

[1] The others are also available from Shearsman: *Square Horizon* in one volume and the other four publications in a compilation volume, *Equatorial and other poems*.

[2] Huidobro always claimed to have published this book first in Buenos Aires in 1916, and at least one purported example of this edition is in the author's papers. The evidence suggests, however—and I say this without having examined the copy in question—that the supposed Buenos Aires edition is a deliberate attempt by Huidobro to antedate his own work in order to "improve" his track record.

Tour Eiffel, was to have a significant impact on the nascent domestic avant-garde in Madrid. Some of the poems were later translated by Huidobro for publication in French magazines, and those versions are also offered here in an appendix.

Together with the experimental French poets, Huidobro was also quickly drawn into the group of expatriate Spanish artists—Picasso, and Juan Gris chief among them. Both Picasso and Gris drew portraits of the poet. The cultural ferment in Paris, despite the war, was something that Huidobro threw himself into. He would soak up the exhibitions, the music—he also got to know the members of Les Six, as well as Edgard Varèse—the literary salons and café society. His work was marked by this forever, although he was to calm down in his artistic maturity after the great long works published in 1931 (*Altazor* and *Temblor de cielo*). He was also to move into other spheres, leaving some of this poetic experimentation behind, writing novels and stage works, repeatedly founding magazines that would quickly fold, while also finding time to join the political fray back in Santiago and, briefly, to run for President.

Like many intellectuals of his era he flirted with leftist politics, and joined the Communist Party—although he was to move away from the Party decisively in later life. He agitated in Madrid in the late 1930s for the Republican government, against Franco's insurrectionist forces.

Huidobro's personal life also went through its ups and downs. During the early years in Paris he was accompanied by his wife, Manuela (1894–1965)—like Vicente, the scion of a Chilean upper-class family—and their children, two born in Chile, and two in Europe. In 1928 he abandoned Manuela in favour of the barely-of-age Ximena Amunátegui (1912–1975), a relative by marriage, whom he whisked away from her boarding school in a dramatic escape to Argentina, whence the pair went to Paris. The couple had one child, Vicente's last. Vicente had been in love with Ximena from 1926, when she was *not* of age, and created an enormous scandal by announcing his infatuation in a long poem that was published in the Santiago newspaper, *La Nación*. Their relationship—not legally binding, as Vicente remained lawfully married to Manuela—lasted officially until 1943 or so, when Ximena left Vicente for a younger admirer, Godofredo Iommi (1917–2001)—another poet, who had been a great fan of Huidobro's work and had been besotted with Ximena since first laying eyes on her; the pair then married. Huidobro's final years were spent in Cartagena, south of Valparaíso on the Chilean coast, with his third "wife"—again, a common-law arrangement—Raquel Señoret, daughter of the late Chilean Ambassador in London.

* * *

As explained above, this volume is one of a series devoted to Huidobro's entire mature poetry, and is also one of three devoted to his work published in that frenetic period in 1917–1918. We expect to make the majority of the author's mature work—and all of the mature poetry—available in translation by 2027.

This second edition of *Arctic Poems* features very few significant changes to the text: three titles have been altered,[3] and some words have been changed here and there in the translations. A few minor errors have also been corrected in both the original languages and the English. What has changed throughout the book, however, is the textual organisation, with this edition now following the 1918 edition for the Spanish texts, and *Saisons choisies* (1921) for most of the French versions in the Appendix. Our previous edition followed the 2003 publication of the author's *Obra poética* in the absence, at that time, of any other good evidence. However, we now have access to a PDF facsimile of the first edition, made available for download by the Biblioteca Nacional de Chile, and I prefer this as a source text, even though, in places, some editorial judgements have still had to be made. The Spanish texts here thus feature all the erratic capitalisation of the original: lines tend to start upper-case, which is normal, but stepped, divided lines sometimes start upper-case, and sometimes not. I have stuck here to the original, slavishly, even where I think it may be wrong, but have used my own judgement as to the best policy regarding capitalisation in the translations. I have increased the leading from our first edition (i.e. made the space between lines greater), but not quite to the extent of the Madrid edition, and have also employed a smaller font-size. This might be regarded as having one's cake and eating it too. Most of the French versions in the Appendix follow the texts in *Saisons choisies* (1921), also made available as a PDF download by the BNC.

Tony Frazer,
March 2025

---

[3] A word of explanation here: two of the titles in the book are in French: 'Gare' and 'Départ'; I originally kept these in French for the English translations, but have now decided to put them into English. I was also wrong to keep the French title, 'Gare' for the translation of the *French* version of that poem.

POEMAS ÁRTICOS

A Juan Gris y Jacques Lipchitz

Recordando nuestras charlas vesperales en aquel rincón de Francia

ARCTIC POEMS

For Juan Gris and Jacques Lipchitz

Remembering our evening conversations in that corner of France

HORAS

El villorio
Un tren detenido sobre el llano

En cada charco
           duermen estrellas sordas
Y el agua tiembla
Cortinaje al viento

                La noche cuelga en la arboleda

En el campanario florecido

Una gotera viva
           Desangra las estrellas

      De cuando en cuando
      Las horas maduras
                  Caen sobre la vida

HOURS

The shanty town
A train halted on the plains

In every puddle
            deaf stars sleep
And the water trembles
Curtain in the wind

                Night hangs in the arboretum

In the overgrown bell tower

A living leak
        bleeds the stars dry

    From time to time
    The ripe hours
                          fall upon life

EXPRÈS

Una corona yo me haría
De todas las ciudades recorridas

    Londres   Madrid   París
    Roma   Nápoles   Zurich

Silban en los llanos
                locomotoras cubiertas de algas

    AQUÍ NADIE HE ENCONTRADO

De todos los ríos navegados
Yo me haría un collar

    El Amazonas   El Sena
    El Támesis   El Rin

Cien embarcaciones sabias
Que han plegado las alas

        Y mi canción de marinero huérfano
        Diciendo adiós a las playas

Aspirar el aroma del Monte Rosa
Trenzar las canas errantes del Monte Blanco
Y sobre el zenit del Monte Cenis
Encender en el sol muriente
El último cigarro

EXPRESS

A crown would I make for myself
Of all the cities I have been through

    London   Madrid   Paris
    Rome   Naples   Zurich

Locomotives covered with seaweed
                              whistle on the plains

    HERE I HAVE FOUND NO ONE

Of all the rivers I have sailed
I would make myself a necklace

      The Amazon   The Seine
      The Thames   The Rhine

A hundred wise vessels
That have folded their wings

           And my orphan sailor's song
           Saying farewell to the shore

Breathing in the scent of Monte Rosa
Braiding the drifting white tresses of Mont Blanc
And on the summit of Mont Cenis
Lighting up my last cigar
In the dying sun

Un silbido horada el aire

    No es un juego de agua

ADELANTE

Apeninos gibosos
                Marchan hacia el desierto

Las estrellas del oasis
Nos darán miel de sus dátiles

En la montaña
El viento hace crujir las jarcias
Y todos los montes dominados
Los volcanes bien cargados
Levarán el ancla

ALLÁ ME ESPERARÁN

Buen viaje

Un poco más lejos
Termina la Tierra

Pasan los ríos bajo las barcas

    La vida ha de pasar

HASTA MAÑANA

A whistle pierces the air

    This is no water game

               ONWARD

Hunchbacked Apennines
              head for the desert

The stars in the oasis
Will give us honey from their dates

On the mountain
The wind makes the rope creak
And all the conquered mountains
The well-loaded volcanoes
Will raise anchor

       THEY WILL WAIT FOR ME THERE

Have a good trip

A little further out
The Earth ends

Rivers pass under the boats

    Life must go on

SEE YOU TOMORROW

NOCHE

Sobre la nieve se oye resbalar la noche

La canción caía de los árboles
Y tras la niebla daban voces

De una mirada encendí mi cigarro

Cada vez que abro los labios
Inundo de nubes el vacío

                         En el puerto
Los mástiles están llenos de nidos

Y el viento
        gime entre las alas de los pájaros

LAS OLAS MECEN EL NAVÍO MUERTO

Yo en la orilla silbando
        Miro la estrella que humea entre mis dedos

NIGHT

Over the snow you can hear the night slip by

The song fell from the trees
And beyond the fog there were voices

With a glance I lit my cigar

Every time I part my lips
I flood the emptiness with clouds

                In the harbour
The masts are full of nests

And the wind
           moans amongst the wings of birds

THE WAVES ROCK THE DEAD SHIP

Whistling on the shore
              I watch the star smoking in my fingers

ALERTA

                                                Media Noche

En el jardín
Cada sombra es un arroyo

Aquel ruido que se acerca no es un coche

Sobre el cielo de París
Otto von Zeppelín

Las sirenas cantan
Entre las olas negras
Y este clarín que llama ahora
No es el clarín de la Victoria

                                               Cien aeroplanos
                                  Vuelan en torno de la luna

            APAGA TU PIPA

Los obuses estallan como rosas maduras
Y las bombas agujerean los días

Canciones cortadas
                      Tiemblan entre las ramas

El viento contorsiona las calles

CÓMO APAGAR LA ESTRELLA DEL ESTANQUE

ALERT

                                              Midnight

In the garden
Every shadow is a stream

That approaching sound is not a car

Over the Paris sky
Otto von Zeppelin

The sirens sing
In the black waves
And this trumpet now calling
Is not the trumpet of Victory

                                A hundred aeroplanes
                                Fly around the moon

        PUT OUT YOUR PIPE

The shells explode like ripe roses
And bombs pierce the days

Songs cut short
                tremble in the branches

The wind leaves the streets writhing

HOW TO SWITCH OFF THE STAR IN THE POND

CAMINO

        Un cigarro en el vacío

A lo largo del camino
He deshojado mis dedos

            Y jamás mirar atrás

Mi cabellera
        Y el humo de esta pipa

Aquella luz me conducía

Todos los pájaros son alas
En mis hombros cantaron

                Pero mi corazón fatigado
                Murió en el último nido

Llueve sobre el camino
Y voy buscando el sitio
            donde mis lágrimas han caído

ROAD

           A cigar in the emptiness

Along the road
I stripped leaves from my fingers

                      and never looked back

My hair
        and the smoke from this pipe

That light guided me

All the wingless birds
Sang on my shoulders

                      But my weary heart
                      Died in the final nest

It's raining on the road
And I go in search of the place
                where my tears have fallen

EMIGRANTE A AMÉRICA

Estrellas eléctricas
Se encienden en el viento

                        Y algunos signos astrológicos
                              Han caído al mar

            Ese emigrante que canta
            Partirá mañana

Vivir
                    Buscar

Atado al barco
              como a un horóscopo
Veinte días sobre el mar

Bajo las aguas
Nadan los pulpos vegetales

Detrás del horizonte
      El otro puerto

Entre el boscaje
Las rosas deshojadas
              iluminan las calles

EMIGRANT TO AMERICA

Electric stars
Switch on in the wind

                        And some astrological signs
                            Have fallen into the sea

          That emigrant who's singing
          Will depart tomorrow

Living
                       Searching

Tied to the ship
          as if to a horoscope
Twenty days at sea

Beneath the waves
Swim the vegetal octopi

Beyond the horizon
      The other harbour

In the thicket
Roses stripped of their petals
                    light up the streets

CANTAR DE LOS CANTARES

Cantar
        Todos los días
                Cantar

Ella vendrá tan rápida
Que su sombra se quedará olvidada
Sin poder encontrar

En el camino
        Las nubes hidrófilas
Se rasgan en las cimas de las hojas

        La lluvia
Detrás del agua
              El sol

Al final de una canción
Alguien doblará los años
                      Y caerá en mis brazos

SONG OF SONGS

Singing
        Every single day
                Singing

She will come so swiftly
That her shadow will remain forgotten
Will not be found again

On the way
        the absorbent clouds
Are ripped open by the tops of the leaves

        Rain
Behind the water
        The sun

At the end of a song
Someone will turn back the years
                and fall into my arms

ASTRO

El libro
        Y la puerta
                Que el viento cierra

Mi cabeza inclinada
                    Sobre la sombra del humo
Y esta página blanca que se aleja

Escucha el ruido de las tardes vivas

      Reloj del horizonte

Bajo la niebla envejecida
Se dirá un astro de resorte

                    Mi alcoba tiembla como un barco

Pero eres tú
            Tú sola
        El astro de mi plafón

Yo miro tu recuerdo náufrago

            Y aquel pájaro ingenuo
            Bebiendo el agua del espejo

STAR

The book
        and the door
                closed by the wind

My head bowed
                over the smoke's shadow
And this white page receding

Listening to the sound of living evenings

      The horizon's clock

Beneath the ageing fog
One would think it a star with springs

                My bedroom shakes like a boat

But it is you
                You alone
        The star in my ceiling rose

I gaze at your shipwrecked memory

                And that gullible bird
                Drinking water from the mirror

NIÑO

Aquella casa
           Sentada en el tiempo
Sobre las nubes
               que alejaba el viento
Iba un pájaro muerto

Caen sus plumas sobre el otoño

Un niño sin alas   { El balandro resbala
Mira en la ventana   Y bajo la sombra de los mástiles
                      Los peces temen trizar el agua

Se olvidó el nombre de la madre

Tras la puerta que bate
                  como una bandera
El techo está agujereado de estrellas

               El abuelo duerme
Cae de su barba
           Un poco de nieve

BOY

That house
            seated in the weather
Above the clouds
               carried away by the wind
Flew a dead bird

Its feathers fall over autumn

A boy with no wings   {   The sloop slips by
Gazes out of the window   And under the shadow of the masts
                           The fish are afraid to pierce the surface

He forgot his mother's name

Behind the door snapping
                like a flag
The roof is riddled with stars

            Grandfather sleeps
From his beard falls
          a bit of snow

CASA

Sobre la mesa
                El abanico tierno
Un pájaro muerto en pleno vuelo

La casa de enfrente
                    blanca de yeso y nieve

En el jardín ignorado
                    Alguien pasea
Y un ángel equivocado
Se ha dormido sobre el humo de la chimenea

                Para seguir el camino
                Hay que recomenzar

      QUIÉN ESCONDIÓ LAS LLAVES

Había tantas cosas que no pude contar

HOUSE

On the table
           the gentle fan
A bird that died in mid flight

The house opposite
                white with plaster and snow

In the abandoned garden
                  someone is walking
And an errant angel
Has fallen asleep over the smoke from the hearth

              To follow the path
              You have to start again

           WHO HID THE KEYS

There were so many things I could not find

RUTA

Última lluvia
                              Los ángeles heridos
                              Dejarán hoy el hospital

He olvidado la canción comenzada

Aquel pájaro que voló de mi pecho
Ha perdido el camino

Bajo los puentes
                el río muere de trecho en trecho

                DÓNDE ESTÁS

Sigue tu marcha tras de mis canciones

La ruta ciega
                como los lagos secos

Todas las estrellas han caído
Y las que cuelgan en las ramas
Caerán también
En el boscaje oblicuo
                Se quedó mi canción

Última lluvia
                              La luna y el pañuelo
                              Se secaban al sol

ROUTE

Final rain
                                      The wounded angels
                                      Will leave hospital today

I have forgotten the song I started

That bird which flew out of my chest
Has lost its way

Under the bridges
                      the river dies one stretch at a time

                    WHERE ARE YOU

Keep walking behind my songs

The path blind
                 as the dry lakes

All the stars have fallen
And those hanging from the branches
Will also fall
In the sloping grove
                    my song remained

Final rain
                                The moon and the handkerchief
                                  Were drying in the sun

GARE

La tropa desembarca
                    En el fondo de la noche

Los soldados olvidaron sus nombres

    Bajo aquel humo cónico
    El tren se aleja como un mensaje telefónico

En las espaldas de un mutilado
Las dos pequeñas alas se han plegado

Y en todos los caminos se ha perdido una estrella

Las nubes pasaron
                Balando hacia el Oriente

Alguien busca su propia huella
Entre las alas olvidadas

Uno
      Dos
           Diez
                Veinte

Y aquella mariposa que jugó entre las flores de los cuadros
Revolotea en torno de mi cigarro

STATION

The troops alight
>   in the dead of night

The soldiers forgot their names

>   Beneath that cone of smoke
>   The train moves away like a telephone call

On a disabled man's back
The two little wings have folded

And on every road a star has been lost

The clouds went by
>   heading eastwards bleating

Someone looks for his own tracks
Amongst the forgotten wings

One
>   Two
>   Ten
>   Twenty

And that butterfly that played amongst the flowers in the paintings
Flits around my cigar

ÉGLOGA

        Sol muriente

Hay una panne en el motor

Y un olor primaveral
Deja en el aire al pasar

          En algún sitio
                    una canción

EN DÓNDE ESTÁS

Una tarde como ésta
        Te busqué en vano

Sobre la niebla de todos los caminos
Me encontraba a mí mismo

Y en el humo de mi cigarro
Había un pájaro perdido

Nadie respondía

        Los últimos pastores se ahogaron

Y los corderos equivocados
Comían flores y no daban miel

ECLOGUE

                Dying sun

There is a fault in the engine

And in passing it leaves behind
A scent of Spring

                Somewhere

                              a song

     WHERE ARE YOU

One evening like this
                I sought you in vain

Above the fog on all the roads
I found my own self

And in the smoke from my cigar
There was a lost bird

No-one answered

                The last shepherds drowned

And the stray lambs
Ate flowers and gave no honey

El viento que pasaba
Amontona sus lanas
                Entre las nubes
                Mojadas de mis lágrimas

A qué otra vez llorar
            lo ya llorado

Y pues que las ovejas comen flores
Señal que ya has pasado

The wind on its way by
Piles up their fleeces
      Among clouds
      Wet with my tears

Why mourn again
      what has already been mourned

And so the sheep eat flowers
A sign that you have already passed by

BALANDRO

Los recuerdos
              se han fatigado de seguirme

        LA SENDA ERA TAN LARGA

Este viento venía de unas alas
Y los días pasan aullando al horizonte

                      Como un balandro joven
                      Crucé muchas tormentas
                      Entre canciones marineras

Todas las gaviotas
                dejaron plumas en mis manos

Tras la última montaña
              los meses descendían

Un póstumo cantar nos cerró la salida

YACHT

Memories
        have tired of following me

        IT WAS SUCH A LONG PATH

This wind was caused by some wings
And the days go howling by to the horizon

                      Like a callow yacht
                      I cruised many storms
                      In between sea shanties

All the gulls
                left feathers in my hands

Behind the final mountain
                the months descended

A posthumous song closed off our exit

INVIERNO

La rubia agreste
                De los ojos trizados
Muerta esta mañana

El invierno pasaba por las calles

Aquel árbol frágil
                guarda todas las lluvias

Estrellas prisioneras
                          Iban
                  Hacia las frías celdas

  Esta llovizna
          Humedece mis pupilas

En un tiempo
           los pájaros cantaron

Y cogieron nuestras manos
Las flores que crecían sobre el río

HAY UNA LUZ
           QUE NOS SOSTIENE DEL VACÍO

WINTER

The blonde country girl
                with the shredded eyes
Dead this morning

Winter wandered the streets

That fragile tree
        holds all the rains

Imprisoned stars
                                  Went
                                To the cold cells

    This drizzle
            moistens my eyes

Once upon a time
                birds sang

And our hands picked
The flowers growing by the river

THERE IS A LIGHT
                KEEPING US FROM THE VOID

HIJO

Las ventanas cerradas
                Y algunas decoraciones deshojadas

      La noche viene de los ojos ajenos

Al fondo de los años
Un ruiseñor cantaba en vano

La luna viva
Blanca de la nieve que caía

Y sobre los recuerdos
                Una luz que agoniza entre los dedos

        MAÑANA PRIMAVERA

Silencio familiar
          Bajo las bujías florecidas

Una canción
        asciende sobre el humo

Y tú
      Hijo
            hermoso como un dios desnudo

Los arroyos que van lejos
Todo lo han visto los arroyos huérfanos

          Un día tendrás recuerdos

SON

The closed windows
                        and some decorations stripped of leaves

      Night comes from the eyes of others

In the depths of the years
A nightingale sang in vain

The living moon
White with snow falling

And over the memories
                        a light extinguished between the fingers

SPRING TOMORROW

Familiar silence
               under the blossoming candles

A song
        rises above the smoke

And you
               my son
                            handsome as a naked god

The streams that flow so far
The orphan streams have seen it all

                One day you will have memories

HORIZONTE

Pasar el horizonte envejecido

Y mirar en el fondo de los sueños
La estrella que palpita

Eras tan hermosa
                    que no pudiste hablar

Y me alejé
            Pero llevo en la mana
Aquel cielo nativo
Con un sol gastado

Esta tarde
           en un café
                      he bebido

                          Un licor tembloroso
                          Como un pescado rojo

Y otra vez en el vaso escondido
Ese sueño filial

Eras tan hermosa
                    que no pudiste hablar

En tu pecho algo agonizaba

HORIZON

Crossing the aged horizon

And gazing into the depths of dreams
The pulsing star

You were so lovely
                you could not speak

I went away
                but I carry in my hand
That native sky
And its worn-out sun

This afternoon
                in a café
                              I have drunk

                              A liquor quivering
                              Like a red fish

And once again in the hidden glass
That filial dream

You were so lovely
                that you could not speak

Something was dying in your breast

Eran verdes tus ojos
                pero yo me alejaba

Eras tan hermosa
                que aprendí a cantar

Your eyes were green
                but I was going away

You were so lovely
                that I learned how to sing

VERMOUTH

Bebo en un café   MONTMARTRE
Al fondo de las horas olvidadas

Vasos de vino ardiente
                 y estrellas fermentadas

TODAS LAS VENDIMIAS
              DE LAS HORAS PASADAS

Una angustia de amor cierra los ojos
Y pesa sobre los sueños este ramo

Llevo los siglos entreabiertos en mis hombros
Llevo todos los siglos y no caigo

Bebedores de vinos rojos
                 Y de cielos gastados

Algo se esconde al fondo de los vasos

Bebedores de mares y de vidas
Yo os doy mi sangre en hostias líricas

Mi sangre que hizo rojas las auroras boreales
Viene de enfermedades vesperales

                         FILIAL LICOR

VERMOUTH

I drink in a café   MONTMARTRE
Deep in the forgotten hours

Glasses of blazing wine
                 and fermented stars

ALL THE VINTAGES
                 OF HOURS GONE BY

Love's despair closes my eyes
And this branch weighs down my dreams

I bear the centuries half-open on my shoulders
I bear all the centuries and I do not fall

Drinkers of red wines
                 and of worn-out skies

Something is hiding at the bottom of the glasses

Drinkers of seas and of lives
I give you my blood in lyrical hosts

My blood that made the Northern Lights red
Comes from evening sicknesses

                          FILIAL LIQUOR

                    Campesinos fragantes
                    Ordeñaban el sol

Los árboles tienen orejas para esta voz que canta
Todos los siglos cantan en mi garganta

    Perfumed peasants
    Were milking the sun

The trees have ears for this voice that sings
All the centuries sing in my throat

LLUEVE

Todo oscuro bajo la lluvia electrizada

La casa
        junto al mar vacío

Y entre los hilos de agua
Se sostiene un nido

            Donde me he ocultado

Sea yo un astro quebrantado
O bien una luciérnaga

Hay mariposas en mi pecho
Y sobre la canción que asciende
Una luz coloniza los desiertos

Esta alondra de nieve se me muere

        UN DÍA PARTIREMOS

Los barcos hacia mares en sordina
Mi estrella hacia la yerba viva

Acaso esta obscuridad
            viene de aquel armario

    EN DONDE ME HE OCULTADO

IT'S RAINING

All dark under the electrified rain

The house
        by the empty sea

And among the trickles of water
There remains a nest

            Where I have gone to hide

Whether I am a fading star
Or even a firefly

There are butterflies in my chest
And above the rising song
A light colonizes the deserts

This snow lark is dying for me

      ONE DAY WE WILL LEAVE

The boats head for muffled seas
My star heads for the living grass

Perhaps this darkness
        comes from that cupboard

      WHERE DID I GO TO HIDE

El patio y la vida llenos de musgos
Del sexto piso
             desciende el ascensor mejor que un buzo

The courtyard and life covered with moss
From the sixth floor
        the elevator comes down better than a diver

ADIÓS

      París

Una estrella desnuda
Se alumbra sobre el llano

                Esa estrella la llevara un mi mano

En Notre Dame
                los ángeles se quejan
Al batir las alas nacen albas
Mas mis ojos se alejan

Todas las mañanas
Baja el sol a tu hostia que se eleva
Y en Montmartre los molinos
                      la atmósfera renuevan

París
En medio de las albas que se quiebran
Yo he florecido tu Obelisco
Y allí canté sobre una estrella nueva

              ADIÓS

Llevo sobre el pecho
Un collar de tus calles luminosas

Todas tus calles
            me llamaban al irme

FAREWELL

    Paris

A naked star
Lights up over the plain

           I will carry that star in my hand

In Notre Dame
        the angels complain
Dawns are born as they beat their wings
But my eyes move away

Every morning
The sun lowers itself to your raised Host
And in Montmartre the windmills
              renew the atmosphere

Paris
Amidst the breaking dawns
I have made your Obelisk bloom
And there I sang above a new star

        FAREWELL

On my chest I wear
A necklace of your shining streets

All your streets
        were calling me as I left

Y en todas las banderas
Palpitaban adioses

Tus banderas de los nobles ardores

Al pasar
 arrojo al Sena
  un ramo de flores

Y entre los balandros que se alejan
Tus balandros que pacen en las tardes
Dejar quisiera el más bello poema

El Sena
 bajo sus puentes se desliza
Y en mi garganta un pájaro agoniza

And on all the flags
Fluttered farewells

Your flags of noble zeal

In passing
        I throw a bunch of flowers
                into the Seine

And among the departing yachts
Your yachts that graze in the afternoons
I would like to leave the most beautiful poem

The Seine
        slips by beneath its bridges
And in my throat a bird is dying

LUNA

Estábamos tan lejos de la vida
Que el viento nos hacía suspirar

    LA LUNA SUENA COMO UN RELOJ

Inútilmente hemos huido
El Invierno cayó en nuestro camino
Y el pasado lleno de hojas secas
Pierde el sendero de la floresta

        Tanto fumamos bajo los árboles
        Que los almendros huelen a tabaco

      Media Noche

Sobre la vida lejana
      Alguien llora
Y la luna olvidó dar la hora

MOON

We were so far away from life
That the wind made us sigh

    THE MOON TICKS LIKE A CLOCK

Needlessly we have fled
Winter fell in our way
And the past full of dry leaves
Loses the woodland path

        We smoke so much beneath the trees
        That the almond trees smell of tobacco

      Midnight

Someone is weeping
        over life far away
And the moon forgot to strike the hour

CRUZ

Algo se ha quedado
Sobre las más tibias lejanías

En todas las rutas
      Había sangre de mis plumas
Al querer recogerlas
       He visto que eran muchas

  No es el Cristo que ha pasado
  Lento como las horas del Oriente

Mi cruz no cargó mis espaldas
Ni vuela sobre los techos

  EN LA CAMPIÑA HABÍA PUNTOS ROJOS

      Mi cruz sin alas iba en mi pecho
      Y no ha querido nunca cerrar los ojos

Un pájaro se quema en el Ocaso

       Cuántas cosas hemos olvidado

Mirando hacia la vida

He visto mi cigarro

      Que humea en las más tibias lejanías

CROSS

Something has remained
Over the most half-hearted distances

On all the roads
                there was blood on my feathers
When I tried to gather them
                    I saw that they were many

        It is not Christ who has passed by
        Slowly as the hours of the Orient

My cross did not overload my back
Nor does it fly over the roofs

    IN THE FIELDS THERE WERE RED SPOTS

            My wingless cross went on my chest
            And has never wished to close its eyes

A bird burns up in the sunset

            How many things we have forgotten

Watching life

I have seen my cigar

        Smoking in the most half-hearted distance

OSRAM

    Dame tus collares encendidos
    Bajo el azul simétrico

En el árbol inverso
                Donde nacen las lluvias

    Un ruiseñor en su cojín de plumas

Tanto batió las alas
                Que desató la nieve

Y los pinos blancos allá sobre los lagos
Eran mástiles reflorecidos

        Jarcias bajo la bruma
        Jarcias entre la espuma

En las olas gastadas
Cuerdas de arpas naufragadas

      ALUMBRA EL FARO BOREAL

Mira las islas que danzan sobre el mar

Nunca fuiste tan bella
Al borde del camino arrojas una estrella

                      VAMOS

Mi clarín llamando hacia los mares árticos
Y tu pupila abierta para todos los náufragos

OSRAM

Give me your burning necklaces
Under the symmetrical blue

In the reversed tree
                where the rains are born

    A nightingale on its feather cushion

Beat its wings so long
                that it loosened the snow

And the white pines there upon the lakes
Were masts blossoming once again

        Rigging beneath the fog
        Rigging amidst the surf

On the spent waves
Strings from shipwrecked harps

    THE NORTHERN BEACON LIGHTS UP

Watch the islands dancing on the sea

You were never so beautiful
At the roadside you throw a star

                  LET'S GO

My bugle calling to the Arctic seas
And your eyes wide open for all shipwrecked souls

PAQUEBOT

He visto una mujer hermosa
Sobre el mar del Norte

Todas las aguas eran su cabellera
Y en su mirada vuelta hacia las playas
Un pájaro silbaba

    Las olas truenan tan roncas
    Que mis cabellos han caído

Recostada sobre la lejanía

Su vientre y su pecho no latían

Sin embargo sus lágrimas vivían

Inclinado sobre mis días
                Bajo tres soles

Miraba allá lejos
El paquebot errante que cortó en dos el horizonte

PACKET BOAT

      I have seen a beautiful woman
      Over the North Sea

All the waters were her tresses
And in the gaze she turned toward the shore
A bird whistled

      The waves thunder and roar so much
      That my hair has fallen out

Lying back over that remote place

Her stomach and her breast did not throb

But her tears still lived

Bent over my days
                beneath three suns

I watched how far away
The roving packet boat cut the horizon in two

MARINO

Aquel pájaro que vuela por primera vez
Se aleja del nido mirando hacia atrás

Con el dedo en los labios
                        Os he llamado

Yo inventé juegos de agua
En la cima de los árboles

Te hice la más bella de las mujeres
Tan bella que enrojecías en las tardes

        La luna se aleja de nosotros
        Y arroja una corona sobre el polo

Hice correr ríos
                que nunca han existido

De un grito elevé una montaña
Y en torno bailamos una nueva danza

        Corté todas las rosas
        De las nubes del Este

Y enseñé a cantar un pájaro de nieve

Marchemos sobre los meses desatados

Soy el viejo marino
                      Que cose los horizontes cortados

SAILOR

That bird on its first flight
Still looking back as it leaves the nest

With a finger to my lips
                        I have called to you

I invented water games
At the tops of trees

I made you the loveliest of women
So lovely that you blushed in the evenings

            The moon recedes from us
            And casts a wreath over the Pole

I made rivers run
                that have never existed before

With a cry I raised a mountain
And we dance a new dance around it

            I cut all the roses
            From the clouds of the East

And I taught a snow bird to sing

Let us leave upon the unleashed months

I am the old sailor
                      who stitches the torn horizons

CENIT

    Lejos de los llanos oblicuos
    Las campanas cantando sobre el cenit

Ayer crucificados en la neblina
Pasé días y días
        Con los brazos abiertos
Entre los barcos que se iban

Donde no encontraré mis huellas

ALGO ME ENCIERRA POR LOS
        CUATRO COSTADOS

La noche

El sacristán equivocado
            Que apagó las estrellas
Rezaba entre las vírgenes de cera

ZENITH

    Far from the sloping plains
    The bells singing above the zenith

Crucified yesterday in the mist
I spent days and days
                  with my arms outstretched
Amongst the departing ships

Where I will not find my tracks

SOMETHING SHUTS ME IN ON ALL
                            FOUR SIDES

By night

The mistaken churchwarden
                        who put out the stars
Prayed amongst wax virgins

NADADOR

Esta noche
        El cielo tan obscuro
Que los cabellos eran sólo humo

En mis dedos hay secretos de alquimia

Apretando un botón
Todos los astros se iluminan

Y tú
    que te alejas cantando entre delfines
Y planetas vivos
                Nadador pensativo
                De todos los jardines

Una tarde traías en tus manos
Cientos de astros enanos

        Nadador pensativo
        Entre la niebla vesperal

Anoche
      La luna enferma murió en el hospital

SWIMMER

Tonight
      the sky so dark
That my hair was just smoke

In my fingers there are alchemical secrets

Pushing a button
All the stars light up

And you
        who go off singing amongst dolphins
And living planets
                Thoughtful swimmer
                Of all the gardens

One evening you bore in your hands
Hundreds of tiny stars

      Thoughtful swimmer
      In the evening mists

Last night
      the ailing moon died in hospital

CUATRO

El mar electrizado
                    Y las piletas de ballenas clavadas

Levando el ancla
Las cuatro estaciones van a la isla de Pascua

           Allí sin florecer me esperas

Al despertar te elevas

Tu vida es una hostia matinal
Y escucho graznar el águila en la roca natal

Entre sombras que pasan
Se desprenden del pecho los recuerdos

                  Esos navíos han levado el ancla

Yo te envío los corderos nativos de mis versos

En medio del Pacífico enmohecido
La Isla de Pascua es un ramo
Que muere todos los años

      ALLÁ EN LA VIDA LOS ADIOSES

Y tú
     desnuda entre tus brazos
Durmiendo sobre cuatro horizontes

FOUR

The electrified sea
                    and pools of trapped whales

Raising anchor
The four seasons go to Easter Island

      You wait for me there without flowering

On waking you rise up

Your life is a morning Host
And I listen to the eagle cry on its birth rock

Among passing shadows
Memories fall away from my chest

                Those ships have raised anchor

I send you the lambs native to my verses

In the midst of the rusty Pacific
Easter Island is a bouquet
That dies every year

      THE FAREWELLS THERE IN LIFE

And you
        naked between your arms
Sleeping on four horizons

DÉPART

        La barca se alejaba
        Sobre las olas cóncavas

De qué garganta sin plumas
                      brotaban las canciones

           Una nube de humo y un pañuelo
           Se batían al viento

Las flores de solsticio
Florecen al vacío
Y en vano hemos llorado
              Sin poder recogerlas

      El último verso nunca será cantado

Levantando un niño al viento
Una mujer decía adiós desde la playa

TODAS LAS GOLONDRINAS SE ROMPIERON LAS ALAS

DEPARTURE

    The boat drifted away
      On the concave waves

From what featherless throat
                      did the songs come forth

          A cloud of smoke and a handkerchief
          Duelled in the wind

The solstice flowers
Bloom in the void
And in vain have we wept
              without being able to pick them

    The final verse will never be sung

Lifting a child to the wind
A woman said farewell from the shore

ALL THE SWALLOWS BROKE THEIR WINGS

DONJON

El castaño en medio del cielo
Palpando como un ciego

Una campana ha llorado
                    sobre el mal y el bien
Los frutos que caen son ovalados
Y las horas también

En la cárcel de enfrente
Las auroras cautivas
                    Cantaban y gemían

Los ahorcados de hace siglos
Al morir miraron los caminos
Donde los otros pasarían

En marcha
                    En marcha

El amor se exalta
Tras la alondra filial de tu garganta

DUNGEON

The chestnut tree in the centre of the sky
Feeling its way like a blind man

A bell has wept
                over good and evil
The fruits that fall are oval
And the hours too

In the prison opposite
The captive dawns
                sang and moaned

The hanged men from centuries past
As they died they saw the paths
That others would walk on

Onward
                              Onward

Love gets excited
Behind the filial lark in your throat

CIGARRO

        Aquello que cae de los árboles
              Es la noche

El mar en mi vaso de aguardiente
Y sobre el mar
        tu sombrero vertical

      A DÓNDE VAS ETERNAMENTE

Alguien ha muerto en tu jardín

La golondrina indiferente
Duerme sobre una cuerda del violín

Yo he tenido en mis manos
        todo lo que se iba

Y esta luna malherida
Indecisa entre el mar y los jardines

Perfumando los años
Una nube montaba de mis labios

Y mi cigarro
        Es la única luz de los confines

CIGAR

        That there falling from the trees
                Is the night

The sea in my brandy glass
And on the sea
        your vertical hat

      WHERE ARE YOU FOREVER GOING

Someone has died in your garden

The unconcerned swallow
Sleeps on a violin string

I have held in my hands
                everything that was leaving

And this injured moon
Unable to choose between sea and gardens

Perfuming the years
A cloud rose from my lips

And my cigar
        is the sole light within these limits

LUNA O RELOJ

Las tardes prisioneras
                             En los rincones fríos

Y las canciones cónicas de los jardines

Golondrinas sin alas
                             Entre la niebla sólida

Angustia en mi garganta

Sobre la frente la corona seca
Y en tus manos una estrella fresca

Después en el valle sin sol
                             Un mismo ruido

La luna y el reloj

MOON OR CLOCK

The evenings imprisoned
                                          in cold corners

And the gardens' conical songs

Wingless swallows
                                          amidst the solid fog

Despair in my throat

On my brow the dry wreath
And in your hands a fresh star

Afterwards in the sunless valley
                                      the very same sound

The moon and the clock

PRIMAVERA

        El poste electrizado
        Orillas del arroyo

Aquel pájaro adormilado
Cantaba como un trompo

    El violinista ha muerto esta mañana
    Pero canta el violín de la ventana

En todas las ramas
Mil canciones mecánicas

Unas venían
        otras se alejaban

LA PRIMAVERA DA VUELTAS AL MANUBRIO

Mas no vimos las notas

Esas alondras
        Anidan en los tubos

La tarde boreal se aleja sobre el humo

SPRINGTIME

      The electrified pole
      Banks of the stream

That dozing bird
Was singing like a top

    The violinist has died this morning
    But the window's violin sings

In all the branches
A thousand mechanical songs

Some came nearer
            others moved away

SPRINGTIME WINDS THE CRANK

But we did not see the notes

Those larks
        nest in the pipes

The northern afternoon moves away over the smoke

ETERNIDAD

Palabras puntiagudas en el azul del viento
Y el enjambre que brilla y que no canta

LA NOCHE EN TU GARGANTA

Acaso Dios se muere
                         Entre almohadones blancos
Bajo el agua gastada de sus párpados

El aire triangular
                para colgar estrellas

Y sobre la verdura nativa de aquel mar

Ir buscando tus huellas
                Sin mirar hacia atrás

ETERNITY

Sharp words in the blue of the wind
And the swarm that shines but does not sing

        THE NIGHT IN YOUR THROAT

Perhaps God is dying
                        amongst white pillows
Under the waste water from his eyelids

The triangular air
                    where stars are hung

And on that sea's natural greenness

Going in search of your tracks
                        without a backward glance

CAMPANARIO

A cada son de la campana
                      Un pájaro volaba

Pájaros de ala inversa
                      Que mueren entre las tejas

Donde ha caído la primera canción

Al fondo de la tarde
                      Las llamas vegetales

En cada hoja tiembla el corazón

Y una estrella se enciende a cada paso

                Los ojos guardan algo
                Que palpita en la voz

Sobre la lejanía
                      Un reloj se vacía

BELL TOWER

Whenever the bell tolled
                        a bird flew by

Birds with reversed wings
                        dying amongst the roof tiles

Where the first song fell

In the depths of the evening
                        the vegetal flames

In every leaf the heart shudders

And a star is switched on with every step

        The eyes retain something
        That throbs in the voice

Over far-off places
                        a clock is emptied out

UNIVERSO

Bajo la enramada
Una canción solidificada

                                      En dónde estamos

El mundo ha cambiado de lugar
Y estrellas falsas brillan en el cielo

          Cordajes de guitarra sobre el mar

La sombra es algo que alza el vuelo

                Junto al arco voltaico
                Un aeroplano daba vueltas

                              En el aire un pañuelo

Y ninguna casa tenía puertas

Un lago oblicuo   El camino sobre
Hace el espacio   el campo inverso

Mañana será el fin del universo

UNIVERSE

Underneath the arbour
A solidified song

                                          Where are we

The world has changed places
And fake stars shine in the sky

            Guitar strings over the sea

The shadow is something that takes flight

                Beside the arc lamp
                An aeroplane was circling

                              A handkerchief in the air

And none of the houses had doors

A sloping lake	The way over
Makes space	The inverted field

Tomorrow will be the end of the universe

EN MARCHA

Cantando se alejaban
                sobre el meridiano

      EN CADA MANO UN NIDO

El vagabundo cotidiano
Recorrió todo el siglo

De los años pasados
                Hicieron sus collares
Tan largos que cruzaban los mares

              Iban buscando el primer día

La sombra de aquel que se quedó perdida
Sobre la ruta la encontré dormida

ADIÓS   ADIÓS

Otro planeta ocupa el sitio del sol

UNDER WAY

They went away singing
                     over the meridian

         A NEST IN EVERY HAND

The everyday vagrant
Roamed the entire century

Out of past years
                they fashioned their necklaces
So long that they crossed the seas

         They went in search of the first day

That man's shadow which went missing
I found it asleep on the road

FAREWELL   FAREWELL

Another planet is taking the sun's place

SOMBRA

La sombra es un pedazo que se aleja
Camino de otras playas

En mi memoria un ruiseñor que se queja

        Ruiseñor de las batallas
        Que canta sobre todas las balas

    HASTA CUÁNDO SANGRARÁN LA VIDA

La misma luna herida
No tiene una ala

            El corazón hizo su nido
            En medio del vacío

Sin embargo
      Al borde del mundo florecen las encinas

Y LA PRIMAVERA VIENE SOBRE LAS GOLONDRINAS

SHADOW

The shadow is a small piece that recedes
On the path to other shores

In my memory a nightingale complaining

      Nightingale of battles
      That sings above all the bullets

    WHEN WILL THEY STOP BLEEDING LIFE

Even the wounded moon
Has only one wing

            The heart made its nest
            Amidst the void

Nonetheless
    holm oaks flourish at the edge of the world

AND SPRINGTIME COMES WITH SWALLOWS

BAY RUM

En tus cabellos se ha dormido
Aquella alondra que voló cantando

      CUÁL ERA MI CAMINO

                    Nunca podré encontrarlo

Las cascadas
        Pequeñas cabelleras en la orilla

Sus estrellas resbalan y no brillan

En el cielo despoblado
Tan solo tu cabellera sideral
Suelta sobre la tarde

      Aquellas llamas que arden
        Oración o cantar

Dame tu mano

Vamos   Vamos

Hay un poco de música en el musgo

Huir
      hacia el último bosque
                    Y en la noche

Vaciar tu cabellera sobre el mundo

BAY RUM

That lark which flew away singing
Has fallen asleep in your hair

        WHICH WAS MY PATH

                      Never will I find it

The waterfalls
        little curls on the shore

Their stars slip by and do not shine

In the deserted sky
Nothing but your astral curls
Let loose over the evening

        Those flames that blaze
        Prayer or song

Give me your hand

Let's go   Let's go

There is a little music in the moss

Fleeing
        to the last woodland
                and in the night

Pouring out your curls over the world

WAGON-LIT

Camino de otras constelaciones
El tren que se desprende de los astros
                              Va cortando la noche

Mis secretos al borde de la almohada

Esta celda errante
                atraviesa los años
Y contra los muros se rompieron mis alas

                              En el aire dos manos

    Tú y yo

Nunca más habrá sol

Mas seguiremos la jornada

Valles
            Selvas
                        Montañas

El invierno
Viene de aquel cementerio

WAGON-LIT

On the way to other constellations
The train that abandons the stars
                          cuts through the night

My secrets on the edge of the pillow

This wandering cell
                    goes through the years
And my wings broke against its walls

                              Two hands in the air

    You and I

Never again will there be sun

But we will continue the day trip

Valleys
                  Forests
                                  Mountains

The winter
Comes from that cemetery

PUERTO

Cruzamiento de alas
           Bajo el cielo nuevo

El azar de los dados en el alma
Y la estrella doméstica que canta

Con las velas al viento
Adónde van mis días
En dónde naufragaron
                    mis naves florecidas

El puerto es una selva que se mece

          Entre mástiles y jarcias
          La alondra momentánea se alejaba

Anclar
        Allá en el aura vesperal

El astro corriente en los arroyos
Ha perdido el piloto

Aquella cabeza flotadora es un escollo

HARBOUR

Crossing wings
        under the new sky

The luck of the dice in the soul
And the home star singing

With sails to the wind
Where do my days go
My flourishing vessels
              where did they founder

The harbour is a forest swaying

        Amongst masts and rigging
        The fugitive lark was leaving

Dropping anchor
            there in the evening breeze

The star flowing in the streams
Has lost the pilot

That floating head is a reef

H P

Pronto llegaremos
Al últimos paralelo

                                        La tarde

   Mi mano
Dirige el automóvil
Igual que un autopiano

                            La estepa en silencio
                            80 caballos de fuerza

                            La estepa

Ir cruzando la tierra

Alguien ha dejado sus alas en el suelo
Y hay golondrinas en tu pecho

Esta mañana
                Cruzaremos las playas

Entre los pájaros vuelan
Las primeras campanadas

Sobre los mares y las primaveras
El barco en que se alejan las mujeres más bellas

HP

We will soon come to
The last parallel

                                        In the afternoon

    My hand
Steers the automobile
Just like a player-piano

                                        The silent plains
                                          80 horsepower

                                          The plains

Crossing the earth

Someone has left his wings on the ground
And there are swallows in your breast

This morning
                                        we will cross the beaches

The first chimes
Fly amongst the birds

Over seas and springtimes
The boat in which the loveliest women leave

VASO

La puerta
        abierta hacia la noche
Y el pájaro sonámbulo en los bosques

Bebe
        Estas auroras rojas

    Los dioses blancos de tu boca
    Ahogándose en el vaso

Aquel mar es tan profundo
Que temblaban los barcos

            Sigamos

Mis ojos entre el humo
Y a la orilla del mundo
Tu mano
        tendida a los naufragios

      Ahora nadie canta

El planeta vacío que dormía en la copa
Está en mi garganta

                Pequeño ruiseñor
POR QUÉ MURIÓ

GLASS

The door
        open to the night
And the sleepwalking bird in the woods

Drinks
        these red dawns

        The white gods of your mouth
        Drowning in the glass

That sea is so deep
That the boats trembled

                Let's go on

My eyes amidst the smoke
And at the edge of the world
Your hand
        extended to the shipwrecks

        Now no one sings

The empty planet which slept in the wine-glass
Is in my throat

                    Little nightingale
WHY DID IT DIE

He buscado en tu cuerpo la canción

Alguien lleva un tesoro entre las manos

        ES UN ASTRO APAGADO
                    O
         UNA ROSA MADURA

Tantas plumas
                Tantas plumas
Y mi pecho desierto
                Ayer henchido de versos

I have searched your body for your song

Someone bears a treasure in his hands

        IT IS A DEAD STAR
                OR
          A RIPE ROSE

So many feathers
                        so many feathers
And my empty breast
                        yesterday swollen with verses

MARES ÁRTICOS

Los mares árticos
                Colgados del ocaso

Entre las nubes se quema un pájaro

Día a día
                Las plumas iban cayendo
Sobre las tejas de todos los tejados

Quién ha desenrollado el arco iris

                        Ya no hay descanso

                Blando de alas
                          Era mi lecho

Sobre los mares árticos

Busco la alondra que voló de mi pecho

ARCTIC SEAS

The Arctic seas
                suspended from the sunset

Among the clouds a bird is burning

Day after day
                the feathers kept falling
Upon the shingles of all the roofs

Who has unwound the rainbow

                There is no more rest

        My bed was
                soft-winged

Over the Arctic seas

I search for the lark that flew from my breast

POEMAS ÁRTICOS

11 versions françaises

publiées en revues &
en *Saisons choisies* (1921)

11 versiones franceses

publicadas en revistas &
en *Saisons choisies* (1921)

ARCTIC POEMS

11 French Versions

published in magazines &
in *Saisons choisies* (1921)

MAISON

Sur la table
           L'éventail si tendre
Un oiseau en plein vol

La maison d'en face
              blanche de chaux et de neige

La vie à l'ombre de la cheminée

Dans le jardin ignoré
        Quelqu'un se promène

Et l'ange bien-aimé
S'est endormi sur la fumée

                    Pour suivre le chemin
                    Il faut recommencer

        QUI A CACHÉ LES CLEFS

Il y avait tant de choses que je ne pus trouver

HOUSE

On the table
            the gentle fan
A bird in full flight

The house opposite
                  white with plaster and snow

Life in the shadow of the hearth

In the abandoned garden
       someone is walking

And the beloved angel
Has fallen asleep over the smoke

                    To follow the path
                    You have to start again

        WHO HAS HIDDEN THE KEYS

There were so many things I could not find

GARE

La troupe débarque
                      Au fond de la nuit

Dans le combat les soldats ont oublié leurs noms

        Sous cette fumée cônique
Le train s'éloigne comme un message téléphonique

Et dans les épaules du poète mutilée
Il y a sûrement deux petites ailes brisées

Sur tous les chemins
                On remarque une étoile de moins

Les nuages passèrent
                    Bêlant vers l'Orient

Tu cherches ta propre empreinte
Parmi les ailes oubliées

Un
      Deux
             Dix
                  Vingt

Et ce papillon qui venait en sleeping-car
Voltige autour de mon cigare

STATION

The troops alight
                in the dead of night

In battle the soldiers forgot their names

        Beneath that conical smoke
The train moves off like a telephone call

And on the shoulders of the maimed poet
There are surely two little broken wings

And on all the roads
                one notices one star less

The clouds went by
                bleating eastwards

You seek your own tracks
Amongst forgotten wings

One
        Two
                Ten
                        Twenty

And that butterfly which came into the sleeping-car
Flits around my cigar

BALANDRE

Les souvenirs sont fatigués de me suivre

      LE SENTIER ÉTAIT SI LONG

Ce vent venait de quelques ailes
Et les jours passent hurlant à l'horizon

        Comme une balandre jeune
        Je traversai toutes les tourmentes
        Parmi des chansons marinières

Toutes les mouettes
      laissèrent des plumes dans mes mains

Derrière la montagne
        les mois descendaient

Tout est parti
Un chant posthume nous ferma la sortie

YACHT

Memories have tired of following me

    THE PATH WAS SO LONG

This wind was caused by some wings
And the days go howling by to the horizon

        Like a callow yacht
        I crossed all the storms
        Surrounded by sea shanties

All the gulls
        left feathers in my hands

Behind the mountain
        the months descended

Everything has gone
A posthumous song closed off our exit

FILS

Les fenêtres fermées
                Et quelques décors effeuillés

       LA NUIT VIENT DES YEUX D'AUTRUI

Au fond des années
En vain le rossignol chantait

La lune vivante
Blanche de la neige qui tombait

Et sur les souvenirs
                  à tout endroit

                Une lumière qui s'éteint entre les doigts

DEMAIN PRINTEMPS

Silence familier
                Sous les bougies en fleur
Une chanson
           s'élève sur la fumée
Et toi
       Mon fils
              beau comme un dieu nu

Les ruisseaux qui s'éloignent
Ils ont tout vu les ruisseaux orphelins

        Sous ton sourire
        Un jour tu auras des souvenirs

SON

The windows closed
                and some decorations stripped of leaves

NIGHT COMES FROM THE EYES OF OTHERS

In the depths of the years
A nightingale sang in vain

The living moon
White with falling snow

And on the memories
                            wherever they might be

              A light snuffed out between the fingers

SPRING TOMORROW

Familiar silence
                under the blossoming candles
A song
       rises above the smoke
And you
           my son
                      handsome as a naked god

The streams that flow away
They have seen it all the orphan streams

            Beneath your smile
            One day you will have memories

LUNE

Nous étions si loin de la vie
Que le vent nous faisait soupirer

    LA LUNE SONNE COMME UN CADRAN

Inutilement nous avons fui
L'hiver tomba sur notre chemin
Et le passé plein de feuilles
Perd le sentier de la forêt

        Nous avons tant fumé sous les arbres
        Que les amandiers sentent le tabac

        Minuit

Sur la vie lointaine
        Quelqu'un pleure

Et la lune oublia de sonner l'heure

MOON

We were so far away from life
That the wind made us sigh

    THE MOON TICKS LIKE A WATCH

Needlessly we have fled
Winter fell in our way
And the past full of leaves
Loses the path in the forest

        We smoked so much beneath the trees
        That the almond trees smell of tobacco

        Midnight

Someone is weeping
        over life far away

And the moon forgot to strike the hour

CIGARE

    Ce qui tombe des arbres
    Est la nuit

La mer dans mon verre d'eau-de-vie
Et sur la mer
        ton chapeau vertical

    OU VAS-TU ÉTERNELLEMENT

Quelqu'un est mort dans ton jardin

L'hirondelle indifférente
Dort sur une corde du violon

J'ai eu dans mes mains
                tout ce qui s'en allait
En cette lune blessée
Indécise entre la mer et les jardins

Parfumant les années
Un nuage montait de mes lèvres

Et mon cigare
        Est l'unique lumière des confins

CIGAR

What falls from the trees
Is the night

The sea in my brandy glass
And on the sea
            your vertical hat

    WHERE ARE YOU FOREVER GOING

Someone has died in your garden

The unconcerned swallow
Sleeps on a violin string

I have held in my hands
                      everything that was leaving
And this injured moon
Unable to choose between sea or garden

Perfuming the years
A cloud rose from my lips

And my cigar
            is the sole light within these limits

ÉTERNITÉ

Des mots pointus dans le bleu du vent
Et l'essaim qui brille y qui ne chante pas

       LA NUIT DANS TA GORGE

Peut-être Dieu meurt
                        Sur ces oreillers blancs
Sous l'aile usée de ses paupières

L'aire triangulaire
                        accrochée aux étoiles

Et sur la verdure native de la mer
Aller cherchant tes traces
                        Sans regarder en arrière

ETERNITY

Sharp words in the blue of the wind
And the swarm that shines but does not sing

    THE NIGHT IN YOUR THROAT

Perhaps God is dying
                            on these white pillows
Under the worn wing of his eyelids

The triangular air
                            suspended from the stars

And on the sea's natural greenness
Going in search of your tracks
                            without a backward glance

CLOCHER

À chaque son des cloches
    Un oiseau s'envole
Oiseaux de métal
     Qui meurent dans las ardoises
OU DONC EST TOMBÉE LA PREMIÈRE CHANSON
Tous les soirs
   Ce feu de joie
Le cœur palpite dans chaque feuille
Et une étoile s'allume à chaque pas
   Les yeux gardent quelque chose
    Qui tremble dans ta voix
Là haut dans la pointe du Zénith
   Il y a une horloge qui se vide

BELL TOWER

Whenever the bell tolled
                a bird took off
Metal birds
        that die on the roof tiles
WHERE IN FACT THE FIRST SONG FELL
Every evening
                this joyous fire
The heart beats in every leaf
And a star is switched on with every step
           The eyes retain something
           That throbs in your voice
Up there at the summit's pinnacle
            there is a clock being emptied out

EN MARCHE

En chantant
                ils s'éloignent sur le méridien

        UN NID DANS CHAQUE MAIN

Le vagabond quotidien
Parcourut tout le siècle

De tous les mois passés
                Ils faisaient des colliers
Si longs qu'ils traversaient les mers

        Ils cherchaient le premier jour
Sur le chemin j'ai trouvé
L'ombre de celui que s'était égaré

    ADIEU
                ADIEU

Une nouvelle planète
          Est à la place du soleil

UNDER WAY

Singing
                they moved away over the meridian

       A NEST IN EVERY HAND

The everyday vagrant
Roamed through the entire century

From all the months past
                      they made necklaces
So long that they crossed the seas

            They went in search of the first day
On the road I found
That man's shadow which had been misplaced

    FAREWELL
                          FAREWELL

A new planet
        is in the sun's place

OMBRE

L'ombre est un morceau qui s'éloigne
Vers d'autres plages
Dans ma mémoire un rossignol se plaint
                Rossignol des batailles
                  Qui chante parmi les balles
       Quand ne saignera-t-on plus la vie
Même la lune blessée
A une seule aile
                Le cœur a fait son nid
                Au milieu du vide
Cependant
    Au bord du monde fleurissent les amandiers
       Et le Printemps vient sur les hirondelles

SHADOW

The shadow is a small piece that recedes
Towards other shores
In my memory a nightingale complaining
          Nightingale of battles
            That sings amongst the bullets
      When will they stop bleeding life
Even the wounded moon
Has only one wing
              The heart has made its nest
           Amidst the void
Nonetheless
    Almond trees flourish at the edge of the world
    And springtime comes with the swallows

BAY RUM

Dans tes cheveux s'est endormie
L'alouette qui s'envola en chantant

    Quel était mon chemin

                  Personne l'a retrouvé

Les cascades
        Des petites chevelures dans la rive
Ces étoiles glissent et ne brillent pas

Dans le ciel dépeuplé
Seulement ta chevelure sidérale
Dénouée sur le soir

            Ces flammes qui montent
            Prière ou chanson

Donné-moi ta main et continuons

Dans le mousse il y a un peu de musique

Fuir
    vers la dernière forêt
              Et dans la nuit

Vider ta chevelure sur l'univers

BAY RUM

The lark that flew away singing
Has fallen asleep in your hair

    Which was my path

           No-one has found it again

The cascades
      of little curls on the shore
These stars slip by and do not shine

In the deserted sky
Nothing but your astral curls
Let loose over the evening

          Those flames that rise
          Prayer or song

Give me your hand and let us carry on

There is a little music in the moss

Fleeing
    to the last forest
        and into the night

Spilling out your curls over the universe

Bibliography

Vicente Huidobro, *Poemas árticos* (Madrid: Imprenta Pueyo, 1918)
Vicente Huidobro, *Saisons choisies* (Paris: Eds. "La Cible", 1921)
Vicente Huidobro (ed.), *Creación* (Madrid, April 1921)
Vicente Huidobro (ed.), *Création* (Paris, November 1921)
Vicente Huidobro, *Obras poéticas en francés* (ed. Waldo Rojas, Santiago: Editorial Universitaria, 1999) [OPF]
Vicente Huidobro, *Obra poética* (ed. Cedomil Goic, Paris: ALLCA XX, 2003) [OP]
Vicente Huidobro, *Poesía reunida* (ed. Vicente Undurraga, Santiago: Ed. Lumen, 2021) [PR]

There are earlier collected editions of the author's work but none are as thorough and dependable as OP. PR is very well presented but manages to leave out all the author's French poems, even when the author's own Spanish translations are available. It thus misrepresents his development, and has basically been *assembled* rather than edited. OPF also leaves out all the author's French versions of his Spanish originals, except where they were part of collections of his poems in French, although two or three do get into the Appendix as "poems published in magazines". The editors of OP were the only ones to attempt an exhaustive survey.

Publication History of the French Versions

'Maison': published in *Saison choisies*, Paris: Eds. "La Cible", 1921.
'Gare': published in *Saison choisies*.
'Balandre': published in *Saison choisies*.
'Fils': published in *Saison choisies*.
'Lune': published in *Saison choisies*.
'Cigare': published in *Saison choisies*.
'Bay Rum': published in *Saison choisies* and previously in the journal *Action*, issue 2:7 (Paris, May 1921). The version printed here is that from *Saisons choisies*.
'Éternité': published in the journal *La Bataille littéraire*, issue 2:6-7 (Paris, 1920). The version here follows the text as printed in the *Obras poéticas en francés*, 1999, as I have not been able to find the magazine issue.

'Clocher': published in the journals *La Bataille littéraire*, issue 2:6-7 and *Creación* (Madrid, April, 1921). The version printed here is that from *Creación*.

'En marche': published in the journal *La Bataille littéraire*, issue 2:6-7. The version here follows the text as printed in the *Obras poéticas en francés*, 1999, as I have not been able to find the magazine issue.

'Ombre': published in the journals *La Bataille littéraire*, issue 2:6-7 and *Création* (Paris, November, 1921). The version printed here is that from *Création*.

A NOTE ON THE TEXTS

I have tried to follow the first edition's layouts wherever possible, although judgement calls were necessary in respect of the exact placement of certain lines, and my font size is smaller and my spacing (i.e. leading) is not quite as generous. As can be seen from the French versions in the Appendix, the poet was not averse to a more cramped style than that used in the 1918 edition of *Poemas árticos*. On the other hand, as we seem to have no statements by the author on such matters, it is quite possible that the typesetters took such decisions into their own hands, although I suspect that the Madrid edition will have followed the author's typescripts fairly closely, as Spanish typesetters were not yet used to the extravagant layouts associated with Apollinaire and others from the new French School of poets. It is also possible that the more cramped style in the Parisian volume owes something to a desire to save space, and paper.

OSRAM
When the poem was written, Osram was the leading European brand of light-bulbs. A German manufacturer founded in 1906, it still exists, with its HQ in Munich.

BAY RUM
Bay Rum was a kind of cologne / aftershave lotion, originating from the Caribbean. Popular in the USA, it became fashionable also in Europe.

WAGON-LIT
A railway sleeping-car, but the term was in common use in English at the time and I have thus retained the phrase in the translation.

www.ingramcontent.com/pod-product-compliance
Lightning Source LLC
Chambersburg PA
CBHW031334160426
43196CB00007B/681